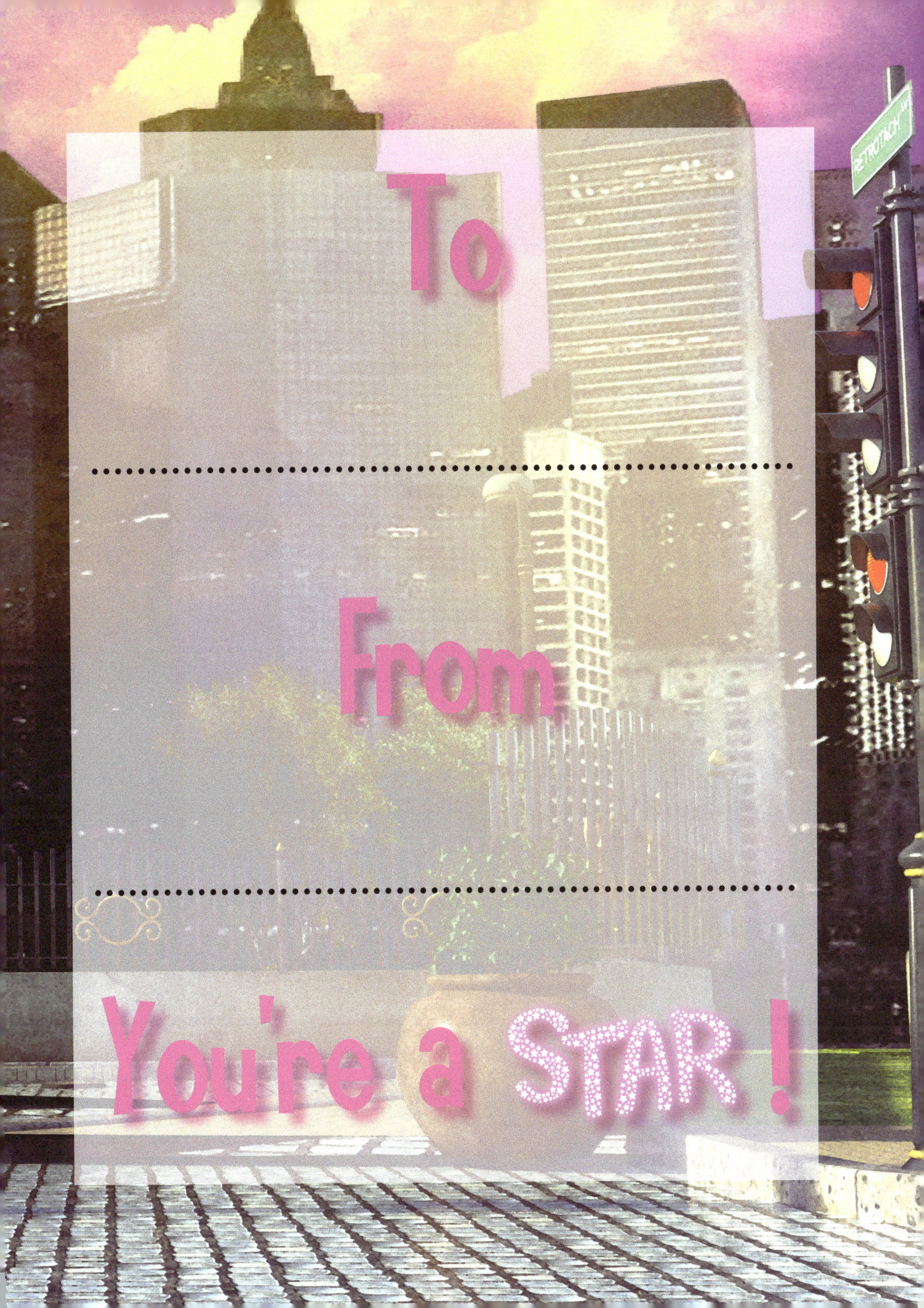
To
From
You're a STAR!

ISBN Hardcover 9781562293031
ISBN eBook 9781562293048

Christian Living Books, Inc.
P. O. Box 7584
Largo, MD 20792
christianlivingbooks.com

Library of Congress Cataloging-in-Publication LCCN 2017060409

Printed in the United States of America

My Uncle Says I'm a STAR

by Muna Heaven

Illustrations by Donna Harriman Murillo

Christian Living BOOKS

Largo, MD

For Savvy — with love,
Mama

Beautiful young minds,

Life will come at you saying, "Your dream is impossible. You don't have IT. You are not enough." I am here to tell you that "you are more than enough! You are God's unique gift. You are more than able to reach your highest dream!"

Along your life's journey, if there is no one around you to cheer you on, know that you always have a fan in me. Be courageous and go for it!!! Dare to dream because dreams DO come true!!!

Your friend,

Dulé Hill

Dulé Hill
Actor, Tap Dancer, Producer

My uncle says I'm a star.

"Beautifully and wonderfully made you are..."

He takes me for long walks.
He likes to tote me up and down.
We make a great pair
Painting the town.

From MoMA to Broadway
A corner diner with pie
I'm pretty sure, I'll always be
The apple of his eye.

I think he thinks he's famous
Because he's always wearing shades.
But I wouldn't trade him for anything-
Not even my favorite roller blades!

My uncle says I'm amazing
That I can be anything I want to be.
Once I put my trust in God
The rest is really up to me.

It won't always be easy.
Truth is, sometimes you might feel down.
But a tap or a song
Can chase those blues right out of town!

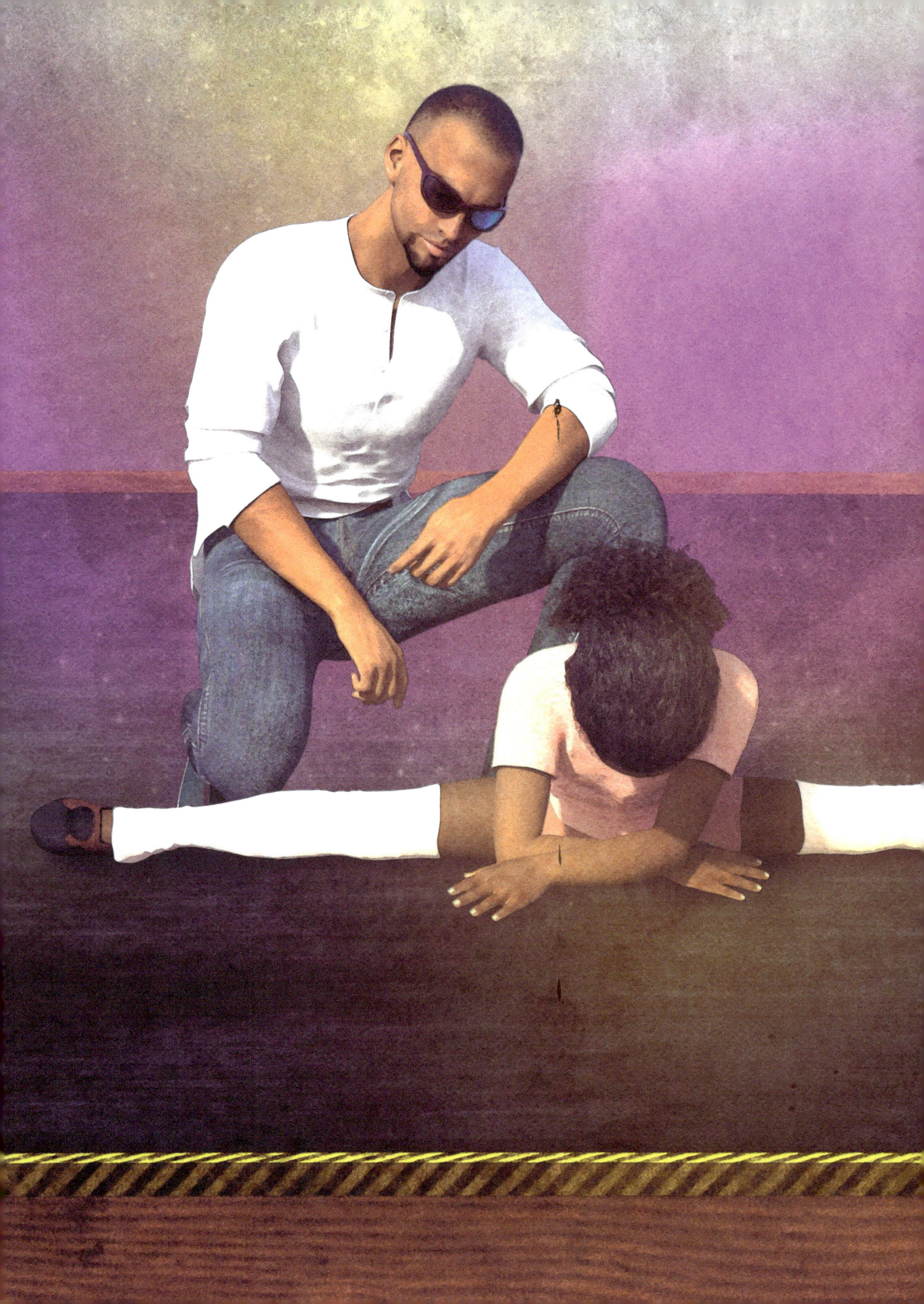

"It doesn't come overnight," he says.
I have to put in the work and the time.
But what a force I will become
Perfecting my purpose - simply sublime!

I can defy the odds.
Yes siree, I can!
If I stay focused on my talents
And let God take care of the plan.

So, I believe in myself.
There's something special about me.
God gave me a gift
For the whole world to see!

I know my uncle loves me
And I really love him too.
I am a growing superstar
Sharing my light with you!

The End

About the Author

MUNA HEAVEN is a Jamaican born, New York-based attorney in family law litigation. She is a graduate of the McGill University Faculty of Law and a Schreyer Honors Scholar graduate from Penn State University. Muna is a past contestant on *The Apprentice* and former equestrian. She is a dedicated mother who also enjoys writing, gardening, and playing music.

Next Book in the Series

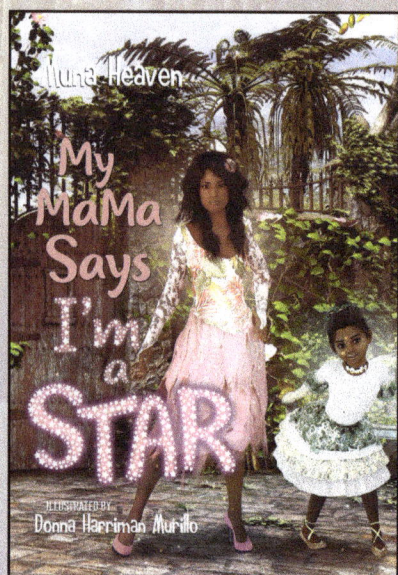

Muna noticed that storybooks lacked characters relatable to her daughter, Savannah (Savvy). With Savvy as her muse, Muna created a series of children's books that speak to the robust empowerment of minority children. The Superstar series addresses essential but oft neglected themes in children's literature including practices of gratitude, belief in self, perseverance, faith, encouragement and love – all vital to bringing out the best in your child – your Superstar. Look for the next book in the series, *My Mama Says I'm a Star*.

DULÉ HILL is an actor, tap dancer and producer. He is best known for his work as Charlie Young on *The West Wing*, for which he garnered an Emmy Award nomination, four Image Award nominations and two Screen Actors Guild Awards. He has been nominated for seven NAACP Image Awards for his work on USA's Psych, in which he portrayed Burton 'Gus' Guster for eight seasons and served as a producer. Dulé was most recently seen portraying Nat "King" Cole in the Patricia McGregor production of *Lights Out: Nat "King" Cole* and in the Tony nominated musical *After Midnight*. Hill first came to prominence opposite Savion Glover and Jeffrey Wright in *Bring in 'Da Noise, Bring in 'Da Funk*.

www.ingramcontent.com/pod-product-compliance
Lightning Source LLC
Chambersburg PA
CBHW040857100426
42813CB00015B/2831